What's gone wrong?

The artist has made some mistakes in this picture.
Can you spot them?

Coloring

Color this picture.

Matching pairs

Draw lines to match the pairs of children's hats.

Cloud maze

Help the plane to get through the maze to the runway.

Crossword

Look at the clues and write your answers in the grid.

1. Where did pizza originally come from? Italy
2. You hear this sound after lightning. thunder
3. Month that comes after March. April
4. If you get sick you go to see one of these.
5. A yellow metal used to make jewelry. gold
6. You look at yourself in one of these.

Dot-to-dot

Starting with number 1, draw a line to join the dots
and complete this picture.

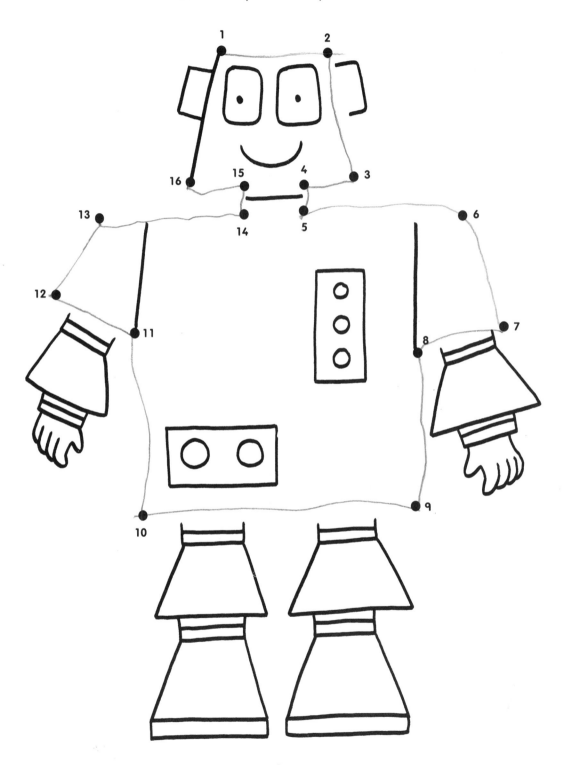

Number puzzle

Fill in the numbers to complete the puzzle. Color the border.

4	+	2	=	6
-	■	×	■	+
1	+	4	=	5
=	■	=	■	=
3	+	8	=	11

4	-	1	=	3
+	■	+	■	+
3	-	1	=	2
=	■	=	■	=
7	-	2	=	5

New words

How many new words can you make from the word tractor?
Write them in the picture.

TRACTOR

Weather wordsearch

The pictures are clues and you will find the words in the grid by reading across or down. Draw a ring around the words.

umbrella

snowman

cloud

sun

rain

S	X	A	U	G	B	O	O	T	S
I	V	K	M	N	O	J	N	R	U
S	A	U	B	Y	C	E	A	T	N
K	A	S	R	A	I	N	O	I	G
A	P	T	E	P	E	I	E	R	L
T	B	C	L	O	U	D	E	A	A
I	Z	X	L	Q	E	N	S	F	S
N	R	A	A	A	U	O	U	N	S
G	S	N	O	W	M	A	N	O	E
B	N	H	Y	T	D	S	A	X	S

sunglasses

boots

skating

- 9 -

Unscramble
Can you unscramble these words? The pictures will help you.

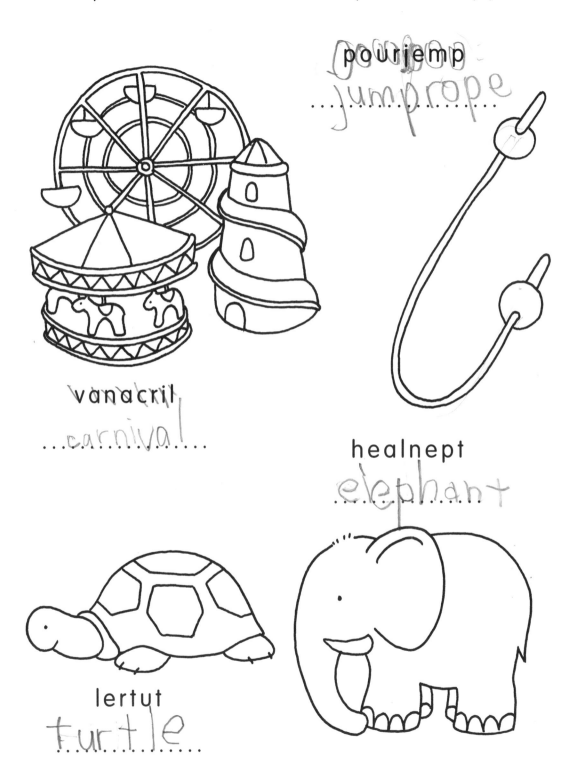

pourjemp

...jumprope...

vanacril

...carnival...

healnept

...elephant...

lertut

...turtle...

Who has what?

Follow the paths to find out which squirrel has the pile of acorns.

What goes together?

Draw lines to match the pictures that go together.

Hidden words

Cross out any letters that appear twice in each box. You will be left with the name of a country.

France

L	F	T	P
R	M	O	A
T	N	M	L
C	P	O	E

Poland

E	U	P	S
O	R	L	E
S	A	U	N
B	R	D	B

Norway

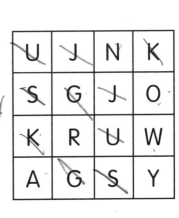

U	J	N	K
S	G	J	O
K	R	U	W
A	G	S	Y

Code

Use this code to work out the secret messages on the following pages.

Secret message

Use the code to break this secret message.

meet me at

the beach

Secret message

Use the code to read the secret message.

let's go to

the movies

Secret message

Use the code to read the secret message.

Where did

you go on

vacation?

Secret message

Break this code to find out the secret message.

Secret message

Use the code to find out the girl's name, and what she likes to read.

Secret message

Break the code, and answer the question.

Secret message

Break this code to find out what is hidden.

Spot the difference

Look carefully at the 2 pictures. Can you spot the differences between them?

Trivia quiz

What does this road sign mean?

a) caution - person opening umbrella

b) road work ahead

c) do not cross the road

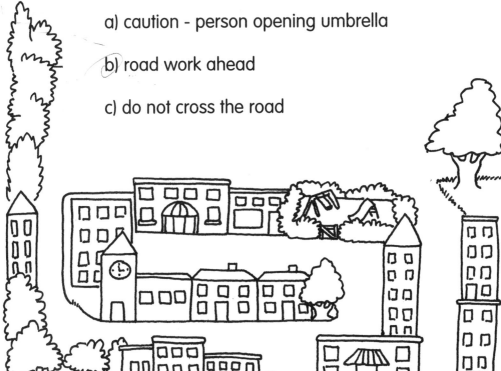

Odd one out

Unscramble the words hidden in the trees. Write the words on the lines. One of the words is the odd one.

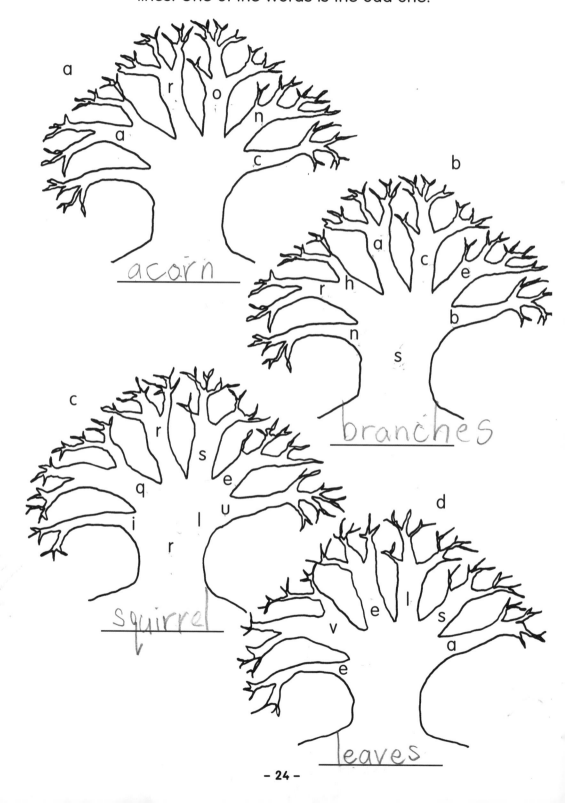

a   r   o   n   a   c

acorn

b   a   c   e   r   h   n   b   s

branches

c   r   s   e   q   u   i   l   r

squirrel

d   e   l   s   v   a   e

leaves

Hidden words

Cross out any letters that appear twice in each box. You will
be left with the name of an animal.

Z	B	X	D
F	G	P	P
E	Z	A	F
D	G	X	R

B	P	B	L
I	M	R	S
A	O	M	P
N	R	A	S

P	M	B	C
O	L	N	K
Q	B	Q	L
E	C	Y	P

Who has what?

Follow the path to find out which child will get to the
ice-cream truck first.

Number puzzle

Fill in the numbers to complete the puzzle. Color the border.

	×	2	=	4
+	■	–	■	+
7	–		=	6
=	■	=	■	=
	+	1	=	

4	×	3	=	
+	■	–	■	–
	×		=	6
=	■	=	■	=
6	+	0	=	

New words

How many new words can you make from the word hippopotamus? Write them in the picture.

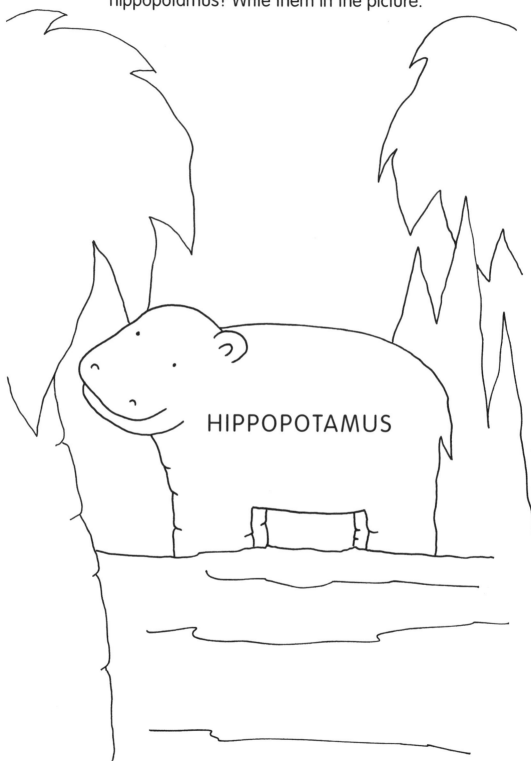

HIPPOPOTAMUS

Crossword

The pictures are clues and the numbers beside them show you where each word goes. Write the words in the grid.

Dot-to-dot

Starting with number 1, draw a line to join the dots and complete this picture.

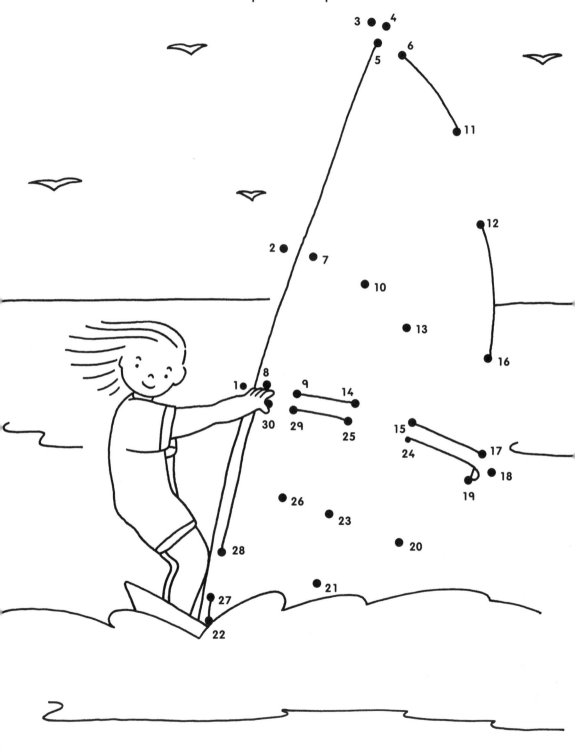

Odd one out
Which one of these animals is the odd one?

Words and pictures

Draw lines to match the pictures of the baby animals with their names.

| foal | piglet | cygnet | duckling |

| lamb | chick |

Coloring
Color this picture.

What's gone wrong?

The artist has made some mistakes in this picture.
Can you spot them?

Matching pairs
Draw lines to match the ties that are the same.

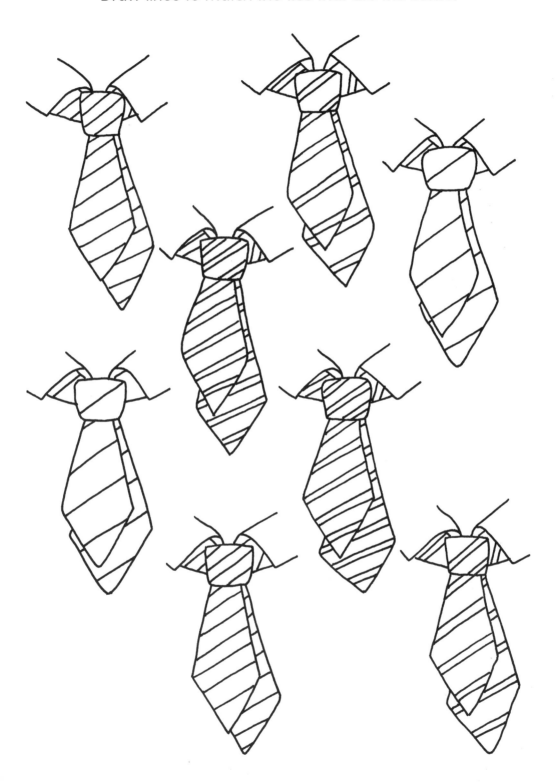

New words

How many new words can you make from the word rainbow?
Write them in the picture.

RAINBOW

Dot-to-dot

Starting with number 1, draw a line to join the dots and complete this picture.

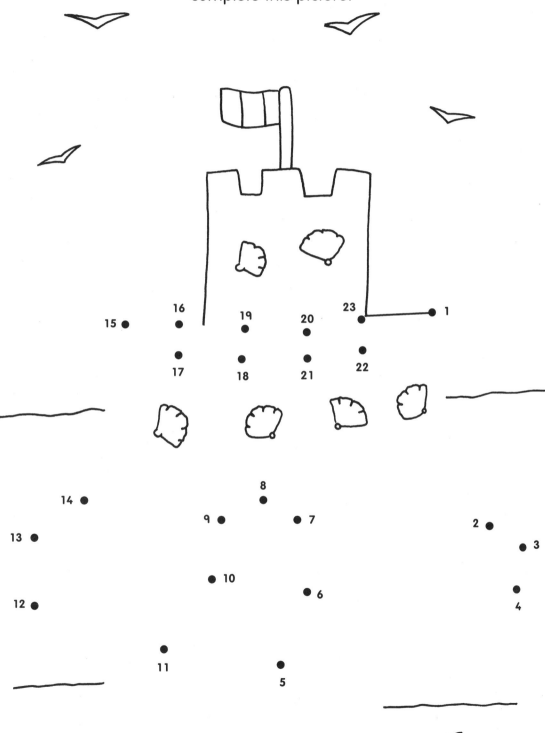

Wordsearch

The pictures are clues and you will find the words in the grid by reading across or down. Draw a ring around the words.

R	T	H	H	E	K	M	N	B	V
C	S	E	E	S	A	W	Z	X	C
F	W	T	Y	H	N	M	O	U	I
K	I	O	P	L	K	B	A	L	L
D	N	D	U	O	K	P	H	V	C
D	G	A	E	Y	S	T	G	H	R
K	L	O	P	L	L	B	R	T	Y
U	I	O	P	I	I	Q	E	D	F
G	H	B	V	C	D	E	R	I	O
K	A	F	R	I	E	N	D	S	A

Crossword

Read the clues, use the pictures to help. Write the answers in the grid.

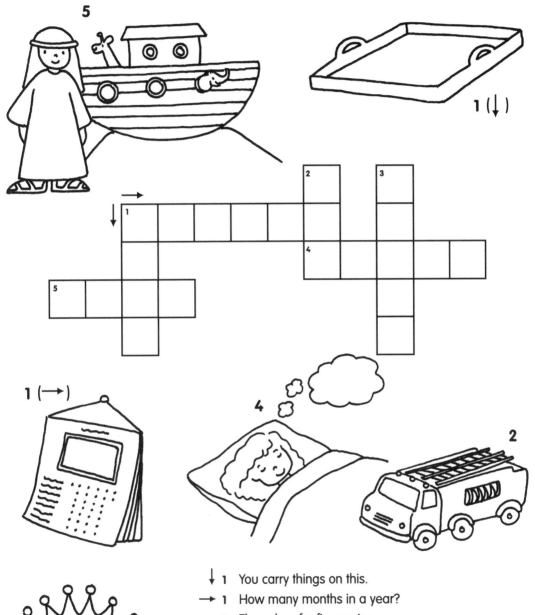

5

1 (↓)

1 (→)

4

2

3

↓ **1** You carry things on this.

→ **1** How many months in a year?

2 The color of a fire engine.

3 She wears a crown.

4 Sometimes when you sleep, you.....

5 He built an ark.

Spot the difference

Look carefully at the 2 pictures. Can you spot the differences between them?

Matching pairs

Draw lines to match the jigsaw pieces which are the same.

Trivia quiz
What is an eagle's nest called?

a) an eyrie

b) a scary

c) a house

What's gone wrong?
The artist has made some mistakes in this picture.
Can you spot them?

CLASS 3

Coloring
Color this picture.

Matching pairs

Draw lines to match the gloves that are the same.

Number puzzle

Fill in the numbers to complete this puzzle. Color the border.

Puzzle 1:

12	+		=	14
−	■	+	■	−
	−	3	=	
=	■	=	■	=
2	+		=	7

Puzzle 2:

	+	4	=	12
−	■	−	■	−
5	+		=	
=	■	=	■	=
	+	3	=	

Who has what?

Follow the lines to find out which child has the biggest kite.

Name the aircraft

Look at the pictures and write the names of the aircraft in the clouds.

biplane	twin engine
helicopter	jumbo jet

What goes together?
Draw lines to match the pictures that go together.

Wordsearch

The pictures are clues and you will find the words in the grid by reading across or down. Draw a ring around the words.

 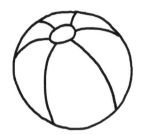 

E	G	L	O	B	E	B	N	H	Y
G	F	D	S	A	B	A	Z	X	C
V	B	N	M	K	A	H	Y	U	I
O	L	P	K	J	L	G	T	R	E
W	M	A	R	B	L	E	H	Y	U
I	O	O	K	M	N	S	M	M	I
S	U	N	J	H	G	F	O	P	R
T	B	N	M	O	O	I	O	O	T
F	C	S	Q	O	R	A	N	G	E
V	F	T	Y	M	N	O	P	D	E

Crossword

The pictures are clues and the numbers beside them show you where each word goes. Write the words in the grid.

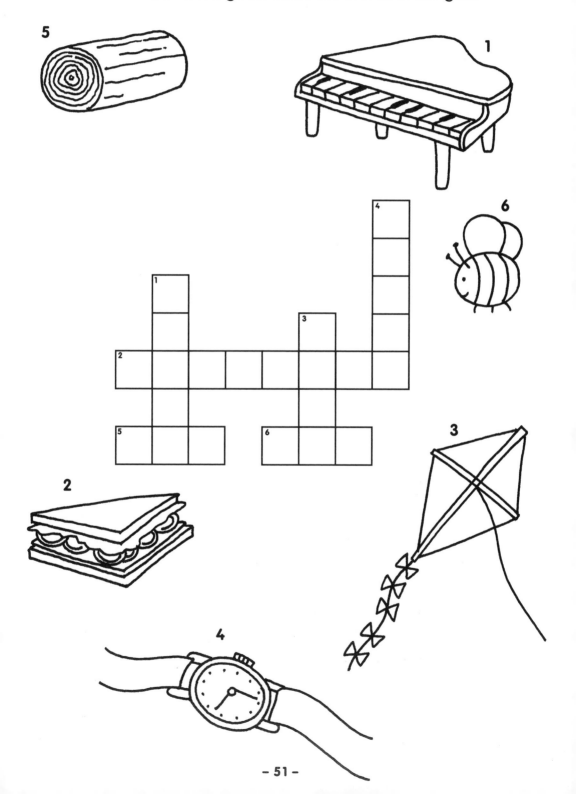

Street maze

Help the fire engine to get through the maze to the fire station.

FIRE STATION

Matching pairs

Draw lines to match the birds that are the same.

Spot the difference

Look carefully at the 2 pictures. Can you spot the differences between them?

Unscramble

Can you unscramble these words? The pictures will help you.

pamlsheda

. . . .

koa eter

. . . .

yackreprss

. . . .

trapie

. . . .

Who does what?

Draw lines from the person to the name of their job. Then link up the picture that goes with the person.

| jockey | gardener | waiter |

Maze

Help the astronaut to get through the maze of stars to the spaceship.

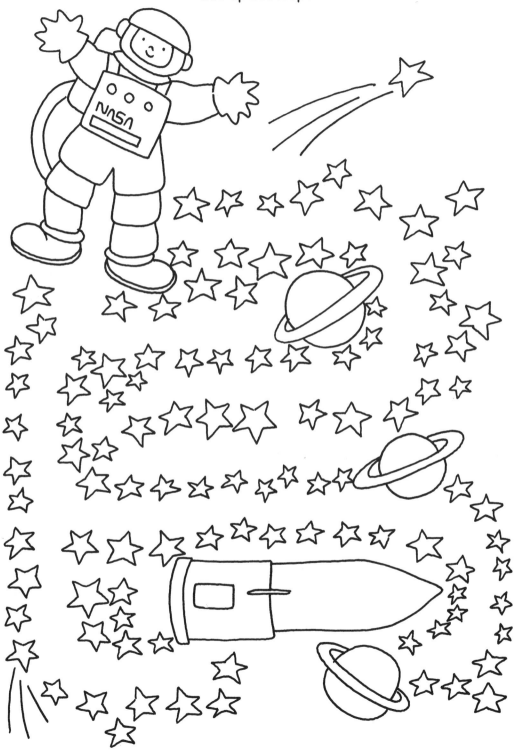

Hidden words

Cross out any letters that appear twice in each box. You will be left with a hidden word.

L	N	O	H
H	R	A	W
O	M	N	G
G	R	W	P

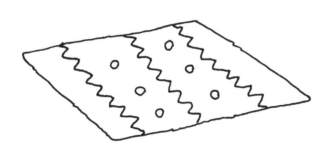

C	H	M	J
X	J	A	H
R	M	O	P
O	E	X	T

V	A	R	D
R	E	B	V
B	L	S	U
U	K	A	L

Dot-to-dot

Starting with number 1, draw a line to join the dots and complete this picture.

Trivia quiz

The British flag is made up of which 3 colors?

a) black, red, yellow

b) blue, yellow, black

c) red, white, blue

Coloring
Color this picture.

Matching pairs

Draw lines to match the boxes that are the same.

Odd one out

Which of these animals is the odd one?

Maze

Help the ancient Egyptian to find his way out of the maze.

Unscramble

Can you unscramble these words? The pictures will help you.

dreinere

. . . .

decrorer

. . . .

yphlxoneo

. . . .

acbuas

. . . .

What's gone wrong?

The artist has made some mistakes in this picture.
Can you spot them?

Maze

Help the young alien to get through the maze to its family.

Crossword

Read the clues, use the pictures to help. Write the answers in the grid.

1 The capital city of France.
2 A baby sheep.
3 These have a lot of pages and you read them.
4 Grass is this color.
5 Which planet are Martians supposed to come from?
6 This planet is very hot and gives Earth its heat and light.

New words

How many new words can you make from the word planet?
Write them in the picture.

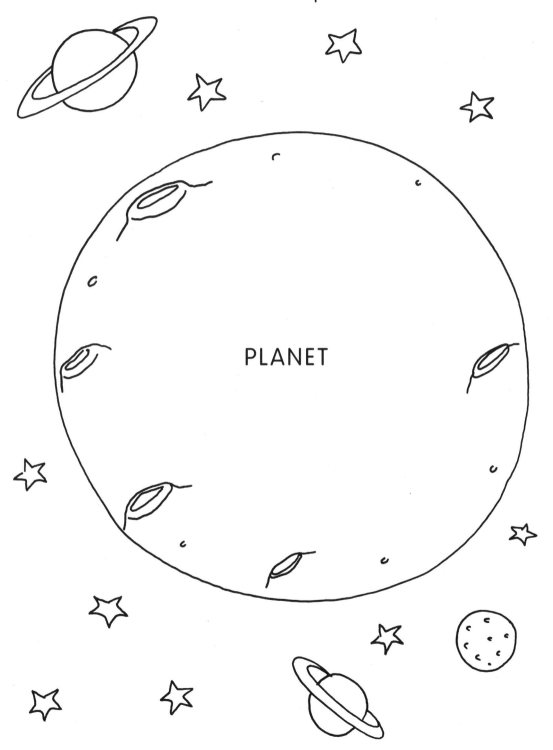

PLANET

Spot the difference

Look carefully at the 2 pictures. Can you spot the differences between them?

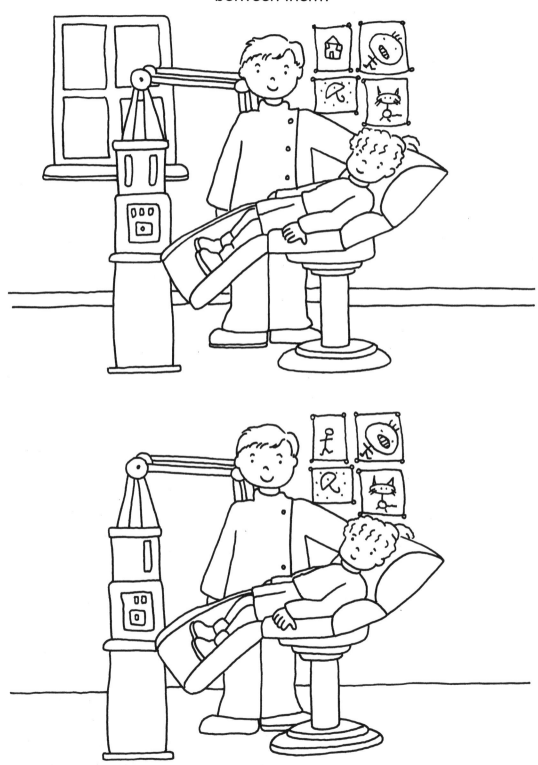

Wordsearch

The pictures are clues and you will find the words in the grid by reading across or down. Draw a ring around the words.

W	E	R	F	D	S	C	V	G	H
B	N	M	J	K	I	I	O	K	C
H	I	G	H	J	U	M	P	D	R
B	N	M	K	A	P	O	I	H	U
H	B	V	F	V	H	U	Y	T	N
X	A	S	W	E	E	F	H	K	N
P	O	R	E	L	A	Y	E	C	I
B	N	M	N	I	L	O	C	O	N
L	I	A	E	N	F	U	I	L	G
G	F	C	M	D	W	P	A	J	X

Dot-to-dot

Starting with number 1, draw a line to join the dots to complete this picture.

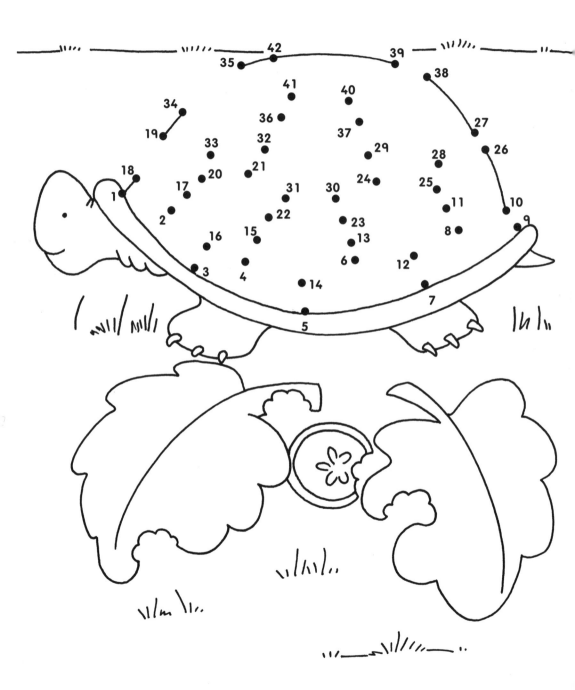

What goes together?

Draw lines to match the pictures that go together.

Crossword

The pictures are clues and the numbers beside them show you where each word goes. Write the words in the grid.

What's gone wrong?

The artist has made some mistakes in this picture.
Can you spot them?

Dot-to-dot

Starting with number 1, draw a line to join the dots and complete this picture.

Number puzzle

Fill in the numbers to complete the puzzle. Color the border.

Puzzle 1:

10	−		=	7
+	■	×	■	−
	÷		=	
=	■	=	■	=
12	−	6	=	

Puzzle 2:

	+	5	=	9
+	■	−	■	+
3	−		=	1
=	■	=	■	=
	+	3	=	

Coloring
Color this picture.

Maze

Help the diver to get through the maze to the treasure.

Odd one out

Which one of these objects is the odd one?

New words

How many new words can you make from the word elephant?
Write them in the picture.

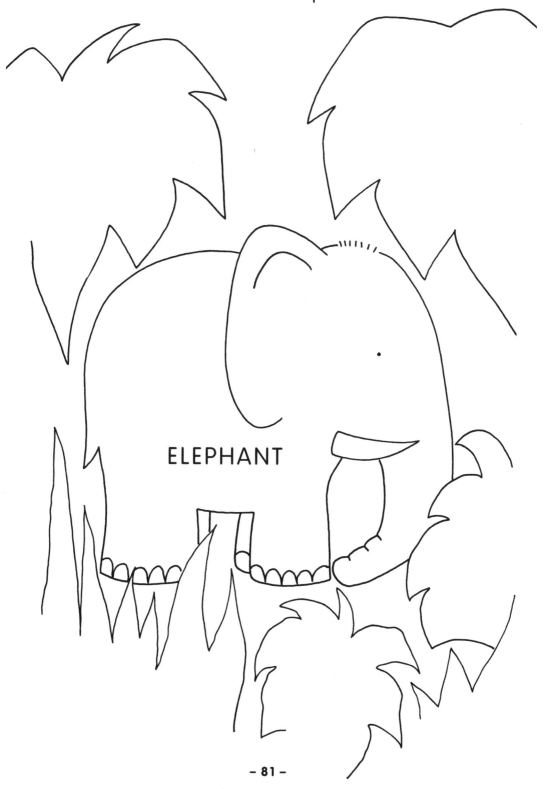

ELEPHANT

What's gone wrong?

The artist has made some mistakes in this picture.
Can you spot them?

Sports wordsearch

The pictures are clues and you will find the words in the grid by reading across or down. Draw a ring around the words.

```
B  T  Y  G  P  J  N  B  V  F
A  X  C  H  O  C  K  E  Y  S
S  U  D  C  L  R  T  Y  U  I
K  E  K  J  O  U  M  U  I  T
E  T  R  D  F  G  B  H  N  E
T  B  A  S  E  B  A  L  L  N
B  A  S  A  W  Y  R  F  G  N
A  O  N  N  O  I  H  G  F  I
L  O  T  Y  V  C  S  A  A  S
L  X  C  P  I  M  H  F  R  D
```

Unscramble

Can you unscramble these words? The pictures will help you.

igwawm

. . . .

tawnierg anc

. . . .

bomariutne

. . . .

kejatc

. . . .

Number puzzle

Fill in the numbers to complete the puzzle. Color the border.

Puzzle 1:

5	+		=	8
+	■	−	■	+
	−		=	
=	■	=	■	=
12	+		=	13

Puzzle 2:

	+	3	=	9
−	■	+	■	−
	−		=	1
=	■	=	■	=
3	+		=	

Dot-to-dot

Starting with number 1, draw a line to join the dots and complete this picture.

New words

How many new words can you make from the word snowman?
Write them in the picture.

SNOWMAN

Pirate's parrot

Follow the lines to find out which pirate has the parrot.

Matching pairs
Draw lines to match the balls that are the same.

Kitten's toy

Follow the lines to find out which kitten has the clockwork mouse.

Number puzzle

Fill in the numbers to complete the puzzle. Color the border.

10	+		=	15
-	■	+	■	-
	-	2	=	
=	■	=	■	=
1	+		=	8

	×	2	=	10
-	■		■	÷
	-		=	2
=	■	=	■	=
2	+		=	

What's gone wrong?

The artist has made some mistakes in this picture.
Can you spot them?

Hidden words

Cross out any letters that appear twice in each box. You will be left with a word.

C	E	F	P
Q	P	O	L
L	I	E	Q
S	O	C	H

M	H	S	O
R	W	A	B
B	N	H	G
S	W	E	M

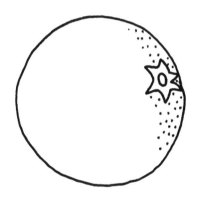

F	A	U	N
K	L	O	Y
Y	U	W	K
N	E	R	A

Unscramble

Can you unscramble these words? The pictures can help you.

oagrknao

. . . .

poptahipmosu

. . . .

liam lost

. . . .

raceswrco

. . . .

Who does what?

Draw lines to join the pictures that go together.

Spot the difference

Look carefully at the 2 pictures. Can you spot the differences between them?

Hidden words

Cross out any letters that appear twice in each box. You will be left with a word.

R	A	M	B
C	I	H	R
M	X	K	X
A	E	H	C

U	M	G	I
Z	B	C	Z
O	G	I	U
M	C	A	T

Q	E	C	O
S	T	V	H
V	I	O	C
T	E	Q	P

Wordsearch

The pictures are clues and you will find the words in the grid by reading across or down. Draw a ring around the words.

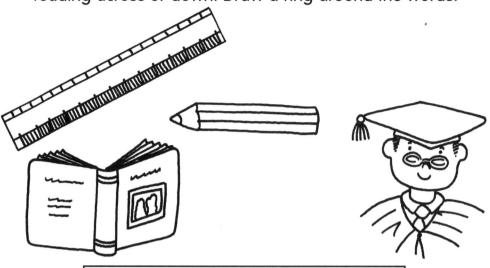

U	I	R	H	G	P	D	S	A	E
R	T	U	G	V	E	N	M	K	C
O	P	L	J	K	N	B	V	C	O
D	P	E	N	S	C	R	T	H	M
U	E	R	L	O	I	M	N	B	P
F	N	D	E	R	L	Y	U	I	U
K	C	H	N	M	B	O	O	K	T
U	I	T	F	E	R	O	K	J	E
B	P	R	O	F	E	S	S	O	R
I	U	R	D	E	R	S	A	A	F

Spot the difference

Look carefully at the 2 pictures. Can you spot the differences between them?

Signposts

Unscramble the names of the countries on the signposts.
Write them on the lines.

_____   _____

_____   _____

_____

Where do they go?

Follow the paths to find out which lane leads to the farmhouse.

a   b   c

Hidden words

Cross out any letters that appear twice in each box. You will be left with a name.

L	P	Q	W
S	M	N	S
A	Q	R	L
W	P	N	K

R	L	Y	J
O	X	U	P
P	I	J	S
Y	R	E	X

Z	K	G	F
F	O	I	H
G	R	O	S
H	T	Z	Y

Trivia quiz

What do the letters PS stand for at the end of a letter?

a) Please Stand

b) Please Sit

c) Post Script

Odd one out

Which one of these animals is the odd one? There is more than one answer.

Spot the difference

Look carefully at the 2 pictures. Can you spot the differences between them?

Mouse maze

Help the mouse to get through the maze to the cheese.

New words

How many new words can you make from the word dinosaur?
Write them in the picture.

DINOSAUR

Answers

1 What's gone wrong?
cat driving car
door on sideways
girl with different pigtails
dog on roller skates
chicken on a leash
window with curtains on outside
person with clothes on back-to-front
lady wearing two different shoes
lamppost with tree branches
car wheel missing

5 Crossword

6 Dot-to-dot
robot

7 Number puzzle

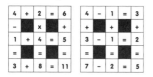

8 New words
TRACTOR
act, art, at, cat, cot, car, carrot, or, rot, rat,
tart, cart, oar, actor, tar
Can you find any more?

9 Wordsearch

```
S L A U G B O O T S
I V K M N O J N R U
S A U B Y C E A T N
K A S R A I N O I G
A P T E P E I E R L
T B C L O U D E A A
I Z X L Q E N S F S
N R A A A U O U N S
G S N O W M A N O E
B N H Y T D S A X S
```

10 Unscramble
carnival
jumprope
turtle
elephant

11 Who has what?
b has the acorns

12 What goes together?
nurse / hospital
firefighter / fire engine
teacher / chalkboard

13 Hidden words
FRANCE
POLAND
NORWAY

15 Secret message
MEET ME AT THE BEACH

16 Secret message
LET'S GO TO THE MOVIES

17 Secret message
WHERE DID YOU GO ON VACATION?

18 Secret message
I LIKE ICE-SKATING

19 Secret message
MARIA ENJOYS READING THE COMICS

20 Secret message
DO YOU LIKE SPORTS?

21 Secret message
THE KEY IS UNDER THE MAT

22 Spot the difference
stripe on man's sweater
ray missing from sun
line missing near top of tower
bird missing
cloud missing
line missing near top of tower
polka dot on girl's pants
line missing near middle of tower
Can you spot any more?

23 Trivia quiz
b) road work ahead

24 Odd one out
acorn
branches

squirrel
leaves
squirrels live in trees, the others grow
on trees

25 Hidden words
BEAR
LION
MONKEY

26 Who has what?
c reaches the ice-cream truck first

27 Number puzzle

2	x	2	=	4		4	x	3	=	12
+		-		+		+		-		-
7	-	1	=	6		2	x	3	=	6
=		=		=		=		=		=
9	+	1	=	10		6	+	0	=	6

28 New words
HIPPOPOTAMUS
pot, top, hip, hop, pop, hat, hot, hit, mat,
mop, must, pat, put, his, has, sat, sit,
ship, shop, soap, post, spot, mast, mash,
math, past, moth, path
Can you find any more?

29 Crossword

30 Dot-to-dot
windsurfer

31 Odd one out
the fish is the only creature that lives
under water

34 What's gone wrong?
zebra behind tree
no windows in house
roof upside down
girl in bathing suit
parrot in tree
rake on end
part of the gate missing

36 New words
RAINBOW
rain, bow, bar, an, row, rob, bin, robin,
ran, won, win, or, on, no, now, rib, brain,
brow, nib, brown, brawn
Can you find any more?

37 Dot-to-dot
sandcastle

38 Wordsearch

```
R T H H E K M N B V
C S E E S A W Z X C
F W T Y H N M O U I
K I O P L K B A L L
D N D U O K P H V C
D G A E Y S T G H R
K L O P L L B R T Y
U I O P I I Q E D F
G H B V C D E R I O
K A F R I E N D S A
```

39 Crossword

							R		Q	
T	W	E	L	V	E		U	
						D	R	E	A	M
N	O	A	H			E	
			Y			N	

40 Spot the difference
face on the sun
cat in the window
bird missing
window missing
girl wearing hat
stripe on bottom of boat
sun missing a ray
pole on top of the boat
Can you spot any more?

42 Trivia quiz
a) an eyrie

43 What's gone wrong?
picture hanging upside down
mouse in mousehole
boy wearing rucksack on his front
teacher's legs facing the wrong direction
teacher wearing graduation cap and gown
spider hanging from fruit machine
girl wearing two watches
girl wearing flippers

46 Number puzzle

12	+	2	=	14		8	+	4	=	12
-		+		-		-		-		-
10	-	3	=	7		5	+	1	=	6
=		=		=		=		=		=
2	+	5	=	7		3	+	3	=	6

47 Who has what?
a has the biggest kite

48 Name the aircraft
jumbo jet
biplane
helicopter
twin-engine

49 What goes together?
horse / stable
bat / belfry
car / garage

50 Wordsearch

51 Crossword

54 Spot the difference
dots missing from books sign
part of window frame missing
sign says closed instead of open
window missing from door
girl wearing skirt
"A" missing from candy sign
bag different shape
button missing from jacket
Can you spot any more?

55 Unscramble
lampshade
oak tree
skyscraper
pirate

56 Who does what?
gardener / wheelbarrow
jockey / horse
waiter / table

58 Hidden words
LAMP
CARPET
DESK

59 Dot-to-dot
balloon

60 Trivia quiz
c) red, white, blue

63 Odd one out
dog is the only pet

65 Unscramble
reindeer
recorder
xylophone
abacus

66 What's gone wrong?
cat sitting in the ocean
moon in the sky
ironing board instead of surfboard
monster in the sea
lady wearing boots
telephone in the sand
lady wearing oven mitts
armchair instead of beach chair

68 Crossword

69 New words
PLANET
an, plant, net, let, lane, ten, plane, pan, tan,
lent, nap, tap, tale, plan, tape, leap, peal,
plate, neat, nape, at, tale, late, ape, ant
Can you find any more?

70 Spot the difference
different picture on wall
button missing on dentist's coat
part of baseboard missing
button missing on machine
line on seat stand missing
dentist's shoes
box missing on machine
window missing
Can you spot any more?

71 Wordsearch

72 Dot-to-dot
turtle

73 What goes together?
knife / fork
paperboy / newspaper
feet / socks
nut and bolt / wrench

74 Crossword

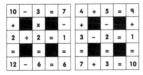

75 What's gone wrong?
boy with a wheelbarrow
seesaw next to pool side
umbrella
lady working at desk
upside-down clock
crab on seesaw
girl holding fish
dolphin in pool

76 Dot-to-dot
camel

77 Number puzzle

10	−	3	=	7		4	+	5	=	9
+		x		−		−		+		+
2	÷	2	=	1		3	−	2	=	1
=		=		=		=		=		=
12	−	6	=	6		7	+	3	=	10

80 Odd one out
trumpet is the only musical instrument

81 New words
ELEPHANT
hat, let, net, pet, pat, pant, pale, ant, ten,
neat, the, tan, an, lent, nap, leap, peal,
heel, tale, help, heap, pea, lean, ale, ape,
hale, pleat, eel, hate, plate
Can you find any more?

82 What's gone wrong?
smoke signals coming out of chimney
black snowball
palm tree
crocodile with ice skates
girl in summer clothes
parrot in tree

83 Wordsearch

84 Unscramble
wigwam
watering can
tambourine
jacket

85 Number puzzle

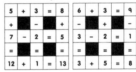

86 Dot-to-dot
truck

87 New words
SNOWMAN
snow, man, now, an, woman, on, sow,
son, won, was, moan, no, nose
How many more can you find?

88 Pirate's parrot
a has the parrot

90 Kitten's toy
a has the clockwork mouse

91 Number puzzle

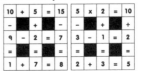

92 What's gone wrong?

basketball instead of a
soccer goal
playing football with a cabbage
boy doing handstand
boy wearing ballet shoes
spectators looking the wrong way
upside-down number 2

93 Hidden words

FISH
ORANGE
FLOWER

94 Unscramble

kangaroo
hippopotamus
mail slot
scarecrow

95 Who does what?

soccer player / soccer ball
zookeeper / elephant
clown / juggling balls
bicyclist / bike

96 Spot the difference

tree trunk missing, left
leaf missing, left
ivy leaf missing
middle tree trunk missing
smaller leaves on right missing
large leaf at front missing
markings on parrot's wing

97 Hidden words

BIKE
BOAT
SHIP

98 Wordsearch

99 Spot the difference

swing missing
face on the sun
handrail missing on the slide

ball missing
girl at bottom of slide
girl in sandpit
polka dots missing on girl's trousers
pail missing
pocket missing on girl by sandbox
Can you spot any more?

100 Signposts

PERU
CHINA
ITALY
SPAIN
FIJI

101 Where do they go?

b leads to the farmhouse

102 Hidden words

MARK
LOUISE
KIRSTY

103 Trivia quiz

c) Post Script

104 Odd one out

zebra is the only animal with stripes
cow is not a wild animal
leopard is the only animal that eats meat

105 Spot the difference

book missing from table
girl's hair
librarian's hair
pattern on girl's sweater
stripe missing on boy's sweater
book missing on shelf
book missing from floor
stripe on librarian's skirt
Can you spot any more?

107 New words

DINOSAUR
din, son, rind, sand, round, nod, so, sun,
in, on, as, an, sound, sin, around, and
Can you find any more?